INTERNATIONAL CONFERENCE ON
SALVAGE (1989)

*FINAL ACT OF THE CONFERENCE
AND CONVENTION ON SALVAGE*

London, 1989

First published in 1989
by the INTERNATIONAL MARITIME ORGANIZATION
4 Albert Embankment, London SE1 7SR
www.imo.org

Printed in the United Kingdom by CPI Books Limited, Reading RG1 8EX

ISBN 978-92-801-1251-1

IMO PUBLICATION
Sales number: I450E

Copyright © International Maritime Organization 1989

All rights reserved.
No part of this publication may be reproduced,
stored in a retrieval system or transmitted in any form
or by any means without prior permission in writing
from the International Maritime Organization.

This publication has been prepared from official documents of IMO, and every effort has been made to eliminate errors and reproduce the original text(s) faithfully. Readers should be aware that, in case of inconsistency, the official IMO text will prevail.

Contents

	Page
Foreword..	v
Final Act of the International Conference on Salvage, 1989...................................	1
International Convention on Salvage, 1989	7
Attachment 1 – Common Understanding concerning Articles 13 and 14 of the International Convention on Salvage, 1989	21
Attachment 2 – Resolution requesting the amendment of the York-Antwerp Rules, 1974	22
Attachment 3 – Resolution on international co-operation for the implementation of the International Convention on Salvage, 1989...................................	23

Foreword

This publication contains the texts of the acts adopted by the International Conference on Salvage, which was held under the auspices of the International Maritime Organization (IMO) from 17 to 28 April 1989.

In addition to the Final Act, the Conference adopted the International Convention on Salvage, 1989. The Conference also adopted a Common Understanding concerning articles 13 and 14 of the Convention, and two resolutions dealing respectively with the amendment of the York-Antwerp Rules of 1974 and international co-operation for the implementation of the 1989 Salvage Convention. The texts of the Common Understanding and the two resolutions are annexed to the Final Act as Attachments 1, 2 and 3.

FINAL ACT OF THE INTERNATIONAL CONFERENCE ON SALVAGE, 1989

1   In accordance with Article 2(b) of the Convention on the International Maritime Organization, the Council of the Organization decided, at its fourteenth extraordinary session in November 1987, to convene an international conference to consider the adoption of a new convention on the law of salvage. This decision was endorsed by the Assembly of the Organization at its fifteenth regular session by resolution A.633(15) of 20 November 1987 on the work programme and budget for the fifteenth financial period 1988-1989.

2   The Conference was held in London, at the Headquarters of the International Maritime Organization, from 17 to 28 April 1989.

3   Representatives of 66 States participated in the Conference, namely the representatives of:

ALGERIA
ARGENTINA
AUSTRALIA
BAHAMAS
BARBADOS
BELGIUM
BRAZIL
BULGARIA
CANADA
CHILE
CHINA
COLOMBIA
CONGO
CÔTE D'IVOIRE
CUBA
CYPRUS
CZECHOSLOVAKIA
DEMOCRATIC PEOPLE'S
  REPUBLIC OF KOREA
DEMOCRATIC YEMEN
DENMARK
ECUADOR
EGYPT
FINLAND
FRANCE
GABON
GERMAN DEMOCRATIC
  REPUBLIC
GERMANY, FEDERAL
  REPUBLIC OF
GHANA
GREECE
HUNGARY
INDIA
INDONESIA
IRAN (ISLAMIC
  REPUBLIC OF)
IRELAND
ISRAEL
ITALY
JAPAN
KIRIBATI
KUWAIT
LIBERIA
MALAYSIA
MARSHALL ISLANDS

MEXICO	SWITZERLAND
MOROCCO	TUNISIA
NETHERLANDS	TURKEY
NIGERIA	UNION OF SOVIET
NORWAY	SOCIALIST REPUBLICS
PANAMA	UNITED KINGDOM OF
PERU	GREAT BRITAIN AND
POLAND	NORTHERN IRELAND
PORTUGAL	UNITED STATES
REPUBLIC OF KOREA	OF AMERICA
SAUDI ARABIA	URUGUAY
SEYCHELLES	VENEZUELA
SPAIN	YUGOSLAVIA
SWEDEN	ZAIRE

4 The following State sent an observer to the Conference:

ROMANIA

5 HONG KONG, an Associate Member of the International Maritime Organization, sent observers to the Conference.

6 A representative of the following body of the United Nations attended the Conference:

OFFICE OF THE UNITED NATIONS HIGH
 COMMISSIONER FOR REFUGEES (UNHCR)

7 The following two intergovernmental organizations sent observers to the Conference:

INTERNATIONAL OIL POLLUTION COMPENSATION
 FUND (IOPC FUND)
ARAB FEDERATION OF SHIPPING (AFS)

8 The following 19 non-governmental international organizations sent observers to the Conference:

INTERNATIONAL CHAMBER OF SHIPPING (ICS)
INTERNATIONAL UNION OF MARINE INSURANCE
 (IUMI)
INTERNATIONAL MARITIME COMMITTEE (CMI)
INTERNATIONAL ASSOCIATION OF PORTS AND
 HARBORS (IAPH)
BALTIC AND INTERNATIONAL MARITIME COUNCIL
 (BIMCO)
LATIN AMERICAN SHIPOWNERS ASSOCIATION (LASA)

OIL COMPANIES INTERNATIONAL MARINE FORUM (OCIMF)
EUROPEAN TUGOWNERS ASSOCIATION (ETA)
INTERNATIONAL SHIPOWNERS' ASSOCIATION (INSA)
FRIENDS OF THE EARTH INTERNATIONAL (FOEI)
INTERNATIONAL ASSOCIATION OF DRILLING CONTRACTORS (IADC)
INTERNATIONAL SALVAGE UNION (ISU)
OIL INDUSTRY INTERNATIONAL EXPLORATION & PRODUCTION FORUM (E & P FORUM)
INTERNATIONAL ASSOCIATION OF INDEPENDENT TANKER OWNERS (INTERTANKO)
INTERNATIONAL GROUP OF P & I ASSOCIATIONS (P & I)
INTERNATIONAL UNION FOR CONSERVATION OF NATURE AND NATURAL RESOURCES (IUCN)
ADVISORY COMMITTEE ON POLLUTION OF THE SEA (ACOPS)
INTERNATIONAL LIFEBOAT FEDERATION (ILF)
INTERNATIONAL ASSOCIATION OF EUROPEAN GENERAL AVERAGE ADJUSTERS (AIDE)

9   His Excellency, Dr. Francisco Kerdel-Vegas, Head of the delegation of Venezuela, was elected President of the Conference.

10   The Vice-Presidents elected by the Conference were:

Rear Admiral F. Lazcano (Chile)
Mr. Meng Guangju (China)
Mr. S. Rosadhi (Indonesia)
Dr. H. Tanikawa (Japan)
Mr. M.M.R. Al-Kandari (Kuwait)
The Rt. Hon. Lord Justice Kerr (United Kingdom of Great Britain and Northern Ireland)
Mr. G.G. Ivanov (Union of Soviet Socialist Republics)
Rear Admiral J.E. Vorbach (United States of America)
Citoyen Tito Yisuku Gafudzi (Zaire)

11   The Secretariat of the Conference consisted of the following officers:

Secretary-General	Mr. C.P. Srivastava Secretary-General of the Organization
Executive Secretary	Mr. T.A. Mensah Assistant Secretary-General

Deputy Executive Secretary	Mr. C.H. Zimmerli, Senior Deputy Director, Legal Affairs and External Relations Division

12   The Conference established a Committee of the Whole with the mandate to consider the draft articles for a Convention on Salvage. The Conference also established a Committee on Final Clauses with the mandate to consider the draft final clauses of the Convention.

13   The Drafting Committee established by the Conference was composed of representatives from the following nine States:

CHINA
EGYPT
FRANCE
MEXICO
NETHERLANDS
SPAIN
UNITED KINGDOM OF GREAT BRITAIN AND NORTHERN IRELAND
UNION OF SOVIET SOCIALIST REPUBLICS
UNITED STATES OF AMERICA

14   A Credentials Committee was appointed to examine the credentials of representatives attending the Conference. The Committee was composed of representatives from the following States:

CONGO
ECUADOR
MALAYSIA
POLAND
SWITZERLAND

15   The officers elected for the Committees were as follows:

Committee of the Whole:

Chairman:	Prof. Dr. N. Trotz (German Democratic Republic)
Vice-Chairmen:	Mr. A. Popp (Canada) Mr. K. Kone (Côte d'Ivoire)

Drafting Committee:

Chairman:	Mr. W.W. Sturms (Netherlands)
Vice-Chairmen:	Mr. J.-P. Béraudo (France) Dr. J. Eusebio Salgado y Salgado (Mexico)

Committee on Final Clauses:

Chairman:	Captain S.A.H. Yafai (Democratic Yemen)
Vice-Chairmen:	Mr. R. Foti (Italy)
	Mr. I. Maku (Nigeria)

Credentials Committee:

Chairman:	Mr. V. Ngayala (Congo)
Vice-Chairman:	Ms. Halimah Ismail (Malaysia)

16 The Conference used as the basis of its work:
- draft articles for a Convention on Salvage, prepared by the Legal Committee of the Organization;
- draft final clauses for the Convention on Salvage, prepared by the Secretariat of the Organization.

17 Also before the Conference were a number of documents, comments and observations, including proposed amendments, submitted by Governments and interested organizations in relation to the draft Convention.

18 As a result of its deliberations based on the reports of the Committee of the Whole, the Committee on Final Clauses and other committees, the Conference adopted the:

International Convention on Salvage, 1989

As far as the French text of this Final Act and of the above-mentioned Convention is concerned, the Conference decided that the term "assistance" means "l'assistance aux navires et le sauvetage des personnes et des biens".

19 The Conference also adopted a Common Understanding concerning articles 13 and 14 of the International Convention on Salvage, 1989 which is contained in attachment 1 to this Final Act.

20 The Conference further adopted the following resolutions:
- Resolution requesting the amendment of the York-Antwerp Rules, 1974
- Resolution on international co-operation for the implementation of the International Convention on Salvage, 1989

These resolutions are contained in attachments 2 and 3 to this Final Act, respectively.

21   This Final Act is established in a single original text in the Arabic, Chinese, English, French, Russian and Spanish languages which is to be deposited with the Secretary-General of the International Maritime Organization.

22   The Secretary-General shall send certified copies of this Final Act with its Attachments and certified copies of the authentic texts of the Convention to the Governments of the States invited to be represented at the Conference, in accordance with the wishes of those Governments.

IN WITNESS WHEREOF the undersigned* have affixed their signature to this Final Act.

DONE IN LONDON this twenty-eighth day of April, one thousand nine hundred and eighty-nine.

---

* Signatures omitted.

INTERNATIONAL CONVENTION ON SALVAGE, 1989

THE STATES PARTIES TO THE PRESENT CONVENTION,

RECOGNIZING the desirability of determining by agreement uniform international rules regarding salvage operations,

NOTING that substantial developments, in particular the increased concern for the protection of the environment, have demonstrated the need to review the international rules presently contained in the Convention for the Unification of Certain Rules of Law relating to Assistance and Salvage at Sea, done at Brussels, 23 September 1910,

CONSCIOUS of the major contribution which efficient and timely salvage operations can make to the safety of vessels and other property in danger and to the protection of the environment,

CONVINCED of the need to ensure that adequate incentives are available to persons who undertake salvage operations in respect of vessels and other property in danger,

HAVE AGREED as follows:

Chapter I
General Provisions

Article 1
Definitions

For the purpose of this Convention:

(a) *Salvage operation* means any act or activity undertaken to assist a vessel or any other property in danger in navigable waters or in any other waters whatsoever.

(b) *Vessel* means any ship or craft, or any structure capable of navigation.

(c) *Property* means any property not permanently and intentionally attached to the shoreline and includes freight at risk.

(d) *Damage to the environment* means substantial physical damage to human health or to marine life or resources in coastal or inland waters or areas adjacent thereto, caused by pollution, contamination, fire, explosion or similar major incidents.

(e) *Payment* means any reward, remuneration or compensation due under this Convention.

(f) *Organization* means the International Maritime Organization.

(g) *Secretary-General* means the Secretary-General of the Organization.

Article 2
Application of the Convention

This Convention shall apply whenever judicial or arbitral proceedings relating to matters dealt with in this Convention are brought in a State Party.

Article 3
Platforms and drilling units

This Convention shall not apply to fixed or floating platforms or to mobile offshore drilling units when such platforms or units are on location engaged in the exploration, exploitation or production of sea-bed mineral resources.

Article 4
State-owned vessels

1   Without prejudice to article 5, this Convention shall not apply to warships or other non-commercial vessels owned or operated by a State and entitled, at the time of salvage operations, to sovereign immunity under generally recognized principles of international law unless that State decides otherwise.

2   Where a State Party decides to apply the Convention to its warships or other vessels described in paragraph 1, it shall notify the Secretary-General thereof specifying the terms and conditions of such application.

Article 5
Salvage operations controlled by public authorities

1   This Convention shall not affect any provisions of national law or any international convention relating to salvage operations by or under the control of public authorities.

2   Nevertheless, salvors carrying out such salvage operations shall be entitled to avail themselves of the rights and remedies provided for in this Convention in respect of salvage operations.

3   The extent to which a public authority under a duty to perform salvage operations may avail itself of the rights and remedies provided for in this Convention shall be determined by the law of the State where such authority is situated.

Article 6
Salvage contracts

1   This Convention shall apply to any salvage operations save to the extent that a contract otherwise provides expressly or by implication.

2   The master shall have the authority to conclude contracts for salvage operations on behalf of the owner of the vessel. The master or the owner of the vessel shall have the authority to conclude such contracts on behalf of the owner of the property on board the vessel.

3   Nothing in this article shall affect the application of article 7 nor duties to prevent or minimize damage to the environment.

Article 7
Annulment and modification of contracts

A contract or any terms thereof may be annulled or modified if:
- (a) the contract has been entered into under undue influence or the influence of danger and its terms are inequitable; or
- (b) the payment under the contract is in an excessive degree too large or too small for the services actually rendered.

Chapter II
Performance of Salvage Operations

Article 8
Duties of the salvor and of the owner and master

1   The salvor shall owe a duty to the owner of the vessel or other property in danger:
- (a)   to carry out the salvage operations with due care;
- (b)   in performing the duty specified in subparagraph (a), to exercise due care to prevent or minimize damage to the environment;
- (c)   whenever circumstances reasonably require, to seek assistance from other salvors; and
- (d)   to accept the intervention of other salvors when reasonably requested to do so by the owner or master of the vessel or other property in danger; provided however that the amount of his reward shall not be prejudiced should it be found that such a request was unreasonable.

2   The owner and master of the vessel or the owner of other property in danger shall owe a duty to the salvor:
- (a)   to co-operate fully with him during the course of the salvage operations;
- (b)   in so doing, to exercise due care to prevent or minimize damage to the environment; and
- (c)   when the vessel or other property has been brought to a place of safety, to accept redelivery when reasonably requested by the salvor to do so.

Article 9
Rights of coastal States

Nothing in this Convention shall affect the right of the coastal State concerned to take measures in accordance with generally recognized principles of international law to protect its coastline or related interests from pollution or the threat of pollution following upon a maritime casualty or acts relating to such a casualty which may reasonably be expected to result in major harmful consequences, including the right of a coastal State to give directions in relation to salvage operations.

Article 10
Duty to render assistance

1   Every master is bound, so far as he can do so without serious danger to his vessel and persons thereon, to render assistance to any person in danger of being lost at sea.

2   The States Parties shall adopt the measures necessary to enforce the duty set out in paragraph 1.

3   The owner of the vessel shall incur no liability for a breach of the duty of the master under paragraph 1.

Article 11
Co-operation

A State Party shall, whenever regulating or deciding upon matters relating to salvage operations such as admittance to ports of vessels in distress or the provisions of facilities to salvors, take into account the need for co-operation between salvors, other interested parties and public authorities in order to ensure the efficient and successful performance of salvage operations for the purpose of saving life or property in danger as well as preventing damage to the environment in general.

Chapter III
Rights of Salvors

Article 12
Conditions for reward

1   Salvage operations which have had a useful result give right to a reward.

2   Except as otherwise provided, no payment is due under this Convention if the salvage operations have had no useful result.

3   This chapter shall apply, notwithstanding that the salved vessel and the vessel undertaking the salvage operations belong to the same owner.

Article 13
Criteria for fixing the reward

1   The reward shall be fixed with a view to encouraging salvage operations, taking into account the following criteria without regard to the order in which they are presented below:

(a) the salved value of the vessel and other property;
(b) the skill and efforts of the salvors in preventing or minimizing damage to the environment;
(c) the measure of success obtained by the salvor;
(d) the nature and degree of the danger;
(e) the skill and efforts of the salvors in salving the vessel, other property and life;
(f) the time used and expenses and losses incurred by the salvors;
(g) the risk of liability and other risks run by the salvors or their equipment;
(h) the promptness of the services rendered;
(i) the availability and use of vessels or other equipment intended for salvage operations;
(j) the state of readiness and efficiency of the salvor's equipment and the value thereof.

2   Payment of a reward fixed according to paragraph 1 shall be made by all of the vessel and other property interests in proportion to their respective salved values. However, a State Party may in its national law provide that the payment of a reward has to be made by one of these interests, subject to a right of recourse of this interest against the other interests for their respective shares. Nothing in this article shall prevent any right of defence.

3   The rewards, exclusive of any interest and recoverable legal costs that may be payable thereon, shall not exceed the salved value of the vessel and other property.

Article 14
Special compensation

1   If the salvor has carried out salvage operations in respect of a vessel which by itself or its cargo threatened damage to the environment and has failed to earn a reward under article 13 at least equivalent to the special

compensation assessable in accordance with this article, he shall be entitled to special compensation from the owner of that vessel equivalent to his expenses as herein defined.

2   If, in the circumstances set out in paragraph 1, the salvor by his salvage operations has prevented or minimized damage to the environment, the special compensation payable by the owner to the salvor under paragraph 1 may be increased up to a maximum of 30% of the expenses incurred by the salvor. However, the tribunal, if it deems it fair and just to do so and bearing in mind the relevant criteria set out in article 13, paragraph 1, may increase such special compensation further, but in no event shall the total increase be more than 100% of the expenses incurred by the salvor.

3   Salvor's expenses for the purpose of paragraphs 1 and 2 means the out-of-pocket expenses reasonably incurred by the salvor in the salvage operation and a fair rate for equipment and personnel actually and reasonably used in the salvage operation, taking into consideration the criteria set out in article 13, paragraph 1(h), (i) and (j).

4   The total special compensation under this article shall be paid only if and to the extent that such compensation is greater than any reward recoverable by the salvor under article 13.

5   If the salvor has been negligent and has thereby failed to prevent or minimize damage to the environment, he may be deprived of the whole or part of any special compensation due under this article.

6   Nothing in this article shall affect any right of recourse on the part of the owner of the vessel.

Article 15
Apportionment between salvors

1   The apportionment of a reward under article 13 between salvors shall be made on the basis of the criteria contained in that article.

2   The apportionment between the owner, master and other persons in the service of each salving vessel shall be determined by the law of the flag of that vessel. If the salvage has not been carried out from a vessel, the apportionment shall be determined by the law governing the contract between the salvor and his servants.

Article 16
Salvage of persons

1 No remuneration is due from persons whose lives are saved, but nothing in this article shall affect the provisions of national law on this subject.

2 A salvor of human life, who has taken part in the services rendered on the occasion of the accident giving rise to salvage, is entitled to a fair share of the payment awarded to the salvor for salving the vessel or other property or preventing or minimizing damage to the environment.

Article 17
Services rendered under existing contracts

No payment is due under the provisions of this Convention unless the services rendered exceed what can be reasonably considered as due performance of a contract entered into before the danger arose.

Article 18
The effect of salvor's misconduct

A salvor may be deprived of the whole or part of the payment due under this Convention to the extent that salvage operations have become necessary or more difficult because of fault or neglect on his part or if the salvor has been guilty of fraud or other dishonest conduct.

Article 19
Prohibition of salvage operations

Services rendered notwithstanding the express and reasonable prohibition of the owner or master of the vessel or the owner of any other property in danger which is not and has not been on board the vessel shall not give rise to payment under this Convention.

Chapter IV
Claims and Actions

Article 20
Maritime lien

1   Nothing in this Convention shall affect the salvor's maritime lien under any international convention or national law.

2   The salvor may not enforce his maritime lien when satisfactory security for his claim, including interest and costs, has been duly tendered or provided.

Article 21
Duty to provide security

1   Upon the request of the salvor a person liable for payment due under this Convention shall provide satisfactory security for the claim, including interest and costs of the salvor.

2   Without prejudice to paragraph 1, the owner of the salved vessel shall use his best endeavours to ensure that the owners of the cargo provide satisfactory security for the claims against them including interest and costs before the cargo is released.

3   The salved vessel and other property shall not, without the consent of the salvor, be removed from the port or place at which they first arrive after the completion of the salvage operations until satisfactory security has been put up for the salvor's claim against the relevant vessel or property.

Article 22
Interim payment

1   The tribunal having jurisdiction over the claim of the salvor may, by interim decision, order that the salvor shall be paid on account such amount as seems fair and just, and on such terms including terms as to security where appropriate, as may be fair and just according to the circumstances of the case.

2   In the event of an interim payment under this article the security provided under article 21 shall be reduced accordingly.

Article 23
Limitation of actions

1   Any action relating to payment under this Convention shall be time-barred if judicial or arbitral proceedings have not been instituted within a period of two years. The limitation period commences on the day on which the salvage operations are terminated.

2   The person against whom a claim is made may at any time during the running of the limitation period extend that period by a declaration to the claimant. This period may in the like manner be further extended.

3   An action for indemnity by a person liable may be instituted even after the expiration of the limitation period provided for in the preceding paragraphs, if brought within the time allowed by the law of the State where proceedings are instituted.

Article 24
Interest

The right of the salvor to interest on any payment due under this Convention shall be determined according to the law of the State in which the tribunal seized of the case is situated.

Article 25
State-owned cargoes

Unless the State owner consents, no provision of this Convention shall be used as a basis for the seizure, arrest or detention by any legal process of, nor for any proceedings *in rem* against, non-commercial cargoes owned by a State and entitled, at the time of the salvage operations, to sovereign immunity under generally recognized principles of international law.

Article 26
Humanitarian cargoes

No provision of this Convention shall be used as a basis for the seizure, arrest or detention of humanitarian cargoes donated by a State, if such State has agreed to pay for salvage services rendered in respect of such humanitarian cargoes.

Article 27
Publication of arbitral awards

States Parties shall encourage, as far as possible and with the consent of the parties, the publication of arbitral awards made in salvage cases.

Chapter V
Final Clauses

Article 28
Signature, ratification, acceptance, approval and accession

1   This Convention shall be open for signature at the Headquarters of the Organization from 1 July 1989 to 30 June 1990 and shall thereafter remain open for accession.

2   States may express their consent to be bound by this Convention by:

   (a) signature without reservation as to ratification, acceptance or approval; or

   (b) signature subject to ratification, acceptance or approval, followed by ratification, acceptance or approval; or

   (c) accession.

3   Ratification, acceptance, approval or accession shall be effected by the deposit of an instrument to that effect with the Secretary-General.

Article 29
Entry into force

1   This Convention shall enter into force one year after the date on which 15 States have expressed their consent to be bound by it.

2   For a State which expresses its consent to be bound by this Convention after the conditions for entry into force thereof have been met, such consent shall take effect one year after the date of expression of such consent.

Article 30
Reservations

1   Any State may, at the time of signature, ratification, acceptance, approval or accession, reserve the right not to apply the provisions of this Convention:

(a)   when the salvage operation takes place in inland waters and all vessels involved are of inland navigation;

(b)   when the salvage operations take place in inland waters and no vessel is involved;

(c)   when all interested parties are nationals of that State;

(d)   when the property involved is maritime cultural property of prehistoric, archaeological or historic interest and is situated on the sea-bed.

2   Reservations made at the time of signature are subject to confirmation upon ratification, acceptance or approval.

3   Any State which has made a reservation to this Convention may withdraw it at any time by means of a notification addressed to the Secretary-General. Such withdrawal shall take effect on the date the notification is received. If the notification states that the withdrawal of a reservation is to take effect on a date specified therein, and such date is later than the date the notification is received by the Secretary-General, the withdrawal shall take effect on such later date.

Article 31
Denunciation

1   This Convention may be denounced by any State Party at any time after the expiry of one year from the date on which this Convention enters into force for that State.

2   Denunciation shall be effected by the deposit of an instrument of denunciation with the Secretary-General.

3   A denunciation shall take effect one year, or such longer period as may be specified in the instrument of denunciation, after the receipt of the instrument of denunciation by the Secretary-General.

Article 32
Revision and amendment

1   A conference for the purpose of revising or amending this Convention may be convened by the Organization.

2   The Secretary-General shall convene a conference of the States Parties to this Convention for revising or amending the Convention, at the request of eight States Parties, or one fourth of the States Parties, whichever is the higher figure.

3   Any consent to be bound by this Convention expressed after the date of entry into force of an amendment to this Convention shall be deemed to apply to the Convention as amended.

Article 33
Depositary

1   This Convention shall be deposited with the Secretary-General.

2   The Secretary-General shall:
- (a) inform all States which have signed this Convention or acceded thereto, and all Members of the Organization, of:
  - (i) each new signature or deposit of an instrument of ratification, acceptance, approval or accession together with the date thereof;
  - (ii) the date of the entry into force of this Convention;
  - (iii) the deposit of any instrument of denunciation of this Convention together with the date on which it is received and the date on which the denunciation takes effect;
  - (iv) any amendment adopted in conformity with article 32;
  - (v) the receipt of any reservation, declaration or notification made under this Convention;
- (b) transmit certified true copies of this Convention to all States which have signed this Convention or acceded thereto.

3   As soon as this Convention enters into force, a certified true copy thereof shall be transmitted by the Depositary to the Secretary-General of the United Nations for registration and publication in accordance with Article 102 of the Charter of the United Nations.

Article 34
Languages

This Convention is established in a single original in the Arabic, Chinese, English, French, Russian and Spanish languages, each text being equally authentic.

IN WITNESS WHEREOF the undersigned* being duly authorized by their respective Governments for that purpose have signed this Convention.

DONE AT LONDON this twenty-eighth day of April one thousand nine hundred and eighty-nine.

---

* Signatures omitted.

ATTACHMENT 1
COMMON UNDERSTANDING CONCERNING ARTICLES 13 AND 14 OF THE INTERNATIONAL CONVENTION ON SALVAGE, 1989

It is the common understanding of the Conference that, in fixing a reward under article 13 and assessing special compensation under article 14 of the International Convention on Salvage, 1989 the tribunal is under no duty to fix a reward under article 13 up to the maximum salved value of the vessel and other property before assessing the special compensation to be paid under article 14.

ATTACHMENT 2
RESOLUTION REQUESTING THE AMENDMENT OF THE YORK-ANTWERP RULES, 1974

THE INTERNATIONAL CONFERENCE ON SALVAGE, 1989,

HAVING ADOPTED the International Convention on Salvage, 1989,

CONSIDERING that payments made pursuant to article 14 are not intended to be allowed in general average,

REQUESTS the Secretary-General of the International Maritime Organization to take the appropriate steps in order to ensure speedy amendment of the York-Antwerp Rules, 1974, to ensure that special compensation paid under article 14 is not subject to general average.

ATTACHMENT 3
RESOLUTION ON INTERNATIONAL CO-OPERATION FOR THE IMPLEMENTATION OF THE INTERNATIONAL CONVENTION ON SALVAGE, 1989

THE INTERNATIONAL CONFERENCE ON SALVAGE, 1989,

IN ADOPTING the International Convention on Salvage, 1989 (hereinafter referred to as "The Convention"),

CONSIDERING IT DESIRABLE that as many States as possible should become Parties to the Convention,

RECOGNIZING that the entry into force of the Convention will represent an important additional factor for the protection of the marine environment,

CONSIDERING that the international publicizing and wide implementation of the Convention is of the utmost importance for the attainment of its objectives,

I   RECOMMENDS:

    (a) that the Organization promote public awareness of the Convention through the holding of seminars, courses or symposia;

    (b) that training institutions created under the auspices of the Organization include the study of the Convention in their corresponding courses of study.

II   REQUESTS:

    (a) Member States to transmit to the Organization the text of the laws, orders, decrees, regulations and other instruments that they promulgate concerning the various matters falling within the scope of application of the Convention;

    (b) Member States, in consultation with the Organization, to promote the giving of help to those States requesting technical assistance for the drafting of laws, orders, decrees, regulations and other instruments necessary for the implementation of the Convention; and

(c) the Organization to notify Member States of any communication it may receive under paragraph II(a).